Book 1
Drawing

By Scott Landowski

&

Book 2
Oil Painting

By Scott Landowski

Book 1
Drawing

By Scott Landowski

1-2-3 Easy Techniques To Mastering Drawing

Drawing: 1-2-3 Easy Techniques to Mastering Drawing

Table of Contents

Introduction

I want to thank you and congratulate you for downloading the book, "Drawing: 1-2-3 Easy Techniques to Mastering Drawing".

This book contains proven steps and strategies on how to master drawing as a beginner artist. You will learn three basic techniques for sketching just about any subject you can think of. These are lines, shading and proportion - that's it!

Anyone can draw. They just need a bit of guidance to know how they can use simple lines and curves to capture the world on paper. There is an artist in each one of us and the tips in this book will help unleash him or her. Start with these techniques and you can move on to creating an art in any medium including painting and digital drawing.

What is important is that you have a good, solid foundation before experimenting with art. After that, you will only be limited by your imagination.

Thank again for downloading this book, I hope you enjoy it!

Chapter 1 - Working with the Right Materials

Like with any other craft, drawing requires the right materials. It is best to choose artist grade and good quality tools, but there are also less expensive options at the art store that can give you real value for your money. Learn to experiment with various brands and types to find the ones that suit you and your drawing style best. There are many wonderful artists who can create beautiful works of art with simple and cheap art tools.

Pencils

Graphite Pencils

First, in order to begin sketching, you must have pencils. You cannot just have any pencil. You need to invest in those with different hardness. The most commonly used type of pencil in sketching is the graphite pencil. Others incorrectly refer to the grey graphite encased inside the wood as lead, when in fact, it has long been banned for use in pencils because it is toxic.

The hardness of a graphite pencil is denoted by a grade that ranges from 9B to 9H. The "B" stands for "black" or graphite that is softer, while "H" stands for graphite that is "harder." The B graphite looks darker while the H graphite is lighter. The HB graphite is the middle ground and it is an absolute must to have. It corresponds to the #2 pencil of more mainstream pencil brands. For sketching, it is often enough to have 5 different pencil grades at your disposal. That is enough to provide different tones and shadows to your drawing.

Other wood pencils can also have colored pigments, or what is pertained to as colored pencils. These, along with graphite pencils, are sharpened using a sharpener that fits the circumference of the pencil.

Mechanical Pencils

You can also use mechanical pencils. These come with barrels that you can refill with graphite of different diameters often denoted by a point millimeter size. You can push out the graphite by pressing a button without the need to sharpen the pencil. They are also excellent for drawing fine details as they retain their point and do not easily become blunt unlike wood pencils.

Pastels

Charcoal and chalk pastels produce colors that are more vivid. They are more blendable than graphite pencils and are also more difficult to control due to their size and softness.

Erasers

Erasers are also just as important as pencils. You can use them not just to correct errors, but to also add highlights and depth to your drawing. Avoid using the eraser found in the body of your pencil. It is often of poor quality and will cause your paper to tear easily. Also, due to its small size, you will quickly grind it down to the wood. A normal rubber eraser will be useful if you want to erase large areas, but you will realize that you will rarely need to do that. If you really do not like your work, it is best to start with a clean sheet of paper. Rubber erasers also create a lot of mess from the grit formed when rubbing them on paper with graphite.

The dust can affect your work and make it dirty. The kneaded artist eraser is much better because it takes off graphite marks without damaging the paper. The eraser lasts longer because rubber bits do not fall off when erasing. You can also erase in layers, which is useful if an area simply needs brightening or highlighting. You can further mold it smaller and pointier to do detail work. As well, a mechanical eraser can target small areas because of its size. You can even sharpen it with a craft knife to create a pointed eraser.

Blenders

Blending tools can help achieve more realistic drawings. The most common is a blending stump, which is a paper or felt cylinder that has been tightly rolled up with pointed ends. Q-tips also serve a similar purpose, but they are meant to be disposable and you cannot use one piece several times. Wads of cotton, paper napkins and fabrics can also be used as blending tools.

Ink

An alternative to sketching with pencils is to use ink. There are even more types of drawing pens than there are pencils. There are artist pens with different millimeter diameters. There are also different types of tips like fine, blunt or scroll (two-tipped). Brush pens, calligraphic pens, nib pens and even markers create various effects in drawing. You can also use a wet brush to spread the ink and color in your drawing. The downside to working with ink is that you can no longer erase your marks. Some artists prefer to draw in pencil first then trace over in ink.

Paper

Drawing paper can greatly affect the outcome of your drawing. However, your choice of brand all comes down to your personal preference. Some prefer paper with pronounced teeth for texture. The teeth refers to the grain of the paper. Pigments stick better to such paper, although the point of your drawing apparatus may also get caught on the teeth. On the other hand, there are those who prefer the look and feel of smoother paper. If you are overwhelmed by the number of paper choices at your disposal, then try to look for paper that was created precisely for pencil sketching.

Watercolor paper also usually makes a good medium for sketching. Avoid paper for acrylics or oils, as well as paper that is similar to fabric like felt and canvas. There are also drawing pads or journals that you can take with you as you travel. Some may prefer to just use notebooks with heavy paper stock for practice drawings.

If you want your drawings to last, you may also want to get a can of fixative. These are usually sprays and they help preserve your drawings. Over time, graphite may transfer or move on the paper, the paper may begin to age and moisture may start to affect the integrity of your drawing. A fixative acts as a protection from possible wear and tear. Think of it as a varnish or a top coat to seal in your work. Remember to purchase a fixative designed mainly for pencils or inks and not for other art media.

Chapter 2 - Warm Up Exercises

If you thought that warming up is just done before physical exercise, then you may be surprised to find out that you must also do warm ups before drawing. You do this to help loosen up your hand and allow you to practice your strokes before doing actual sketching.

Grip

First, warm up exercises help reorient you on how to hold your pencil properly. Many people are used to gripping their pencil for sketching the way they do for writing where it is nestled on top of the gap between their thumb and forefinger, so the bottom is pointing up. This is called the tripod grip. The best way to hold your pencil for sketching is to position it underneath the palm of your hand in what is called the overhand grip. This type of grip is looser and allows you bigger movement that comes from your entire arm rather than just your wrist. Also, you will not be smudging your paper because your hand hovers on top of the paper.

Doodles

Start by doing slanted lines. Quickly draw lines that move diagonally up then diagonally down. Do rows of this and draw them as fast as you can, then as close together as possible. Make them even and the same size every time.

Sketch hatches that are crossed horizontal and vertical lines.

Next, draw curved lines or Cs. Draw them forward, then in reverse. Just like the slanted lines, make them even and in rows.

From there, move on to doing spirals or ovals one on top of the other. Draw rows of perfect circles afterwards.

Draw 3D shapes. You can start by sketching cubes. Shade the exposed surfaces in different tones to practice your shading and shadows.

Sketch cylinders and bowls and shade them in using curved strokes, as well. Do the same for cones.

Contour Drawing

Also, do some contour drawing. Pick an object and draw its outline without lifting your pencil off your paper. This teaches you to pay attention to the shape of the object you are drawing. Some artists also like doing this exercise without looking at their paper, so their full attention is on the subject itself. If you want to have a bit more challenge, turn your back from your paper and draw without looking back. This is best done on a large paper like an A3 size. This exercise is what you call a blind contour.

Do not be occupied with making your warm up drawings perfect. You can just do them on scratch paper and sketch as many exercises as you want, although you also need to start practicing control. Remember that you are not simply doing. The warm up exercises are more purposeful than that and they will help you perform your strokes better later on when you are already doing actual sketches.

Chapter 3 - Choosing Subjects

Even though you want to draw abstract art or highly stylized figures, it is still important to learn how to draw objects realistically. This will teach you proper proportions and shadows. Once you have mastered realistic drawing, you will be able to break conventions and develop your own style.

Still Life

Beginner art classes usually start by sketching still life, which refers to small inanimate objects. You can just find random objects lying around your home or inside your bag. Try to find a combination of different textures, shapes and sizes. For example, a towel, bottle and fruits will allow you to practice drawing different types of objects. Also, make sure to arrange them in a way that they occupy different levels (i.e., high and low) and depths of fields (i.e., foreground, middle ground and background). This will teach you scale and perspective.

The most important thing to focus on when drawing still life is shape. For instance, an apple is just a circle with slight curves to make it look distinct from an orange. Likewise, a bottle is just a cylinder while a towel is just a polygonal shape. Once you can see shapes in real life, then it will be easier to capture how objects look in your sketches.

From small objects, you can move on to larger things like furniture or even entire rooms. The practice in perspective will also help you transition to doing landscapes.

Landscape

What is most important in landscape is perspective. You may have seen landscape paintings where most of the details are blurred. This is completely understandable, because when you are drawing something vast like a mountain view or an urban jungle, you won't be able to draw all the small parts. The observer won't notice these in real life when they are looking at the bigger picture. However, when there is something off with your perspective, then the illusion of realism is shattered.

For example, a tree close to the viewer should be bigger than a large mountain that is miles away. Amateur artists who do not pay attention to what they can actually see in the world may not realize this because in real life, trees are much smaller than mountains, but sometimes, what you think is logical does not really match reality.

Figure Drawing

This is especially true when drawing people. You may instinctively think that your leg is longer than your arm when they are actually the same length. Your ears are also not high on your head but right in the middle of it at the same level as your nose.

Some artists start with statues, so you can go to an art gallery or a park where there are busts and sculptures. Look for subjects with realistic proportions. Again, focus on the shapes that you can find in a human body. The head is a circle while the limbs are cylinders. Spend more time on getting the actual figure or overall shape of the subject before learning how to draw the fingers, toes and facial features. Portraits or faces are typically the last type of drawings that artists master.

Next, you can practice drawing actual people. You can have a model sit down for a session or discreetly draw strangers sitting down in a public place.

There are places that offer figure drawing sessions with professional models. Some do nude modeling, which is beneficial for artists who want to understand fully how the human body looks.

Gesture Drawing

Gesture drawings are done quickly, usually in short intervals of 15, 30 or 60 seconds, with the use of expressive lines and shapes. They serve as starting points for different genres of art that do not rely on hyper-realistic figures like impressionism. Gesture drawings focus on the basic form and proportion of a subject and record that without much emphasis on details. They are good for practicing speed and expressing movement in drawing. Erasing is rarely done and mistakes give the drawing even more character.

The subject of a gesture drawing can be any object in motion like moving persons, animals, cars, boats and toys. The best place to find subjects is outdoors where there are lots of activities. You can watch a busy intersection and try to draw different kinds of people walking about and dodging cars. In a park, you can draw joggers with their dogs or children playing with their toys.

Chapter 4 - Easy Technique 1 - Lines

For any drawing that you do, you can start with an H pencil to create light outlines and follow up with a B pencil for the darker, more defined lines. However, you can also simply use just one pencil and vary your pressure as you draw more layers of lines. Also, the point of your pencil, especially when freshly sharpened, will create thin, light lines.

On the other hand, the side of your pencil will create thick, dark lines. You can also make the point blunt by rubbing it on another piece of paper. If you want to just use one pencil, instead of switching between H and B pencils, then use an HB or #2 pencil as described in Chapter 1.

So, your drawing should have at least two layers of lines: the first light outline, which you can use as a guideline to capture the basic shapes of the subject, and thicker lines on top of that to form the rest of your drawing.

For the first layer of lines, try to use a light pressure when pressing down on your pencil and use only light strokes. The fainter you make the lines, the better. They will be easier to erase later on if you have to.

The layer on top of the outline will use heavy lines. You can trace over the light outline, then vary your pressure and strokes as you go along to create more definition to your figure. Define the edges and the details. At this point, you want to be more careful as erasing may be more difficult to do on thick, dark lines. Even if you can lift the marks off your paper, the indentations may still be obvious and they may show up more if you draw over them.

You can also go over your final pencil outlines with ink and erase the pencil lines for a more polished look.

In drawing, it is impossible to create perfectly straight lines, so do not worry if your tables or boxes have crooked edges. The only way to achieve truly straight lines is to use a ruler, although dragging or rolling your pencil on its edge, instead of using the point, will help achieve straighter lines. Also, imperfect lines give your drawings more life and expression. Perfectly straight lines are also difficult to find in nature and in real life. Even buildings or straight poles have curves and small dips on their edges. That is why a drawing that makes use of straight lines looks cold, stiff and lifeless. It looks rather unrealistic and uninteresting.

Lines and Values

Drawings are made up of lines and clusters of lines or values. Lines are the flowing strokes of a pencil that define edges or small details while values are used to define the form and design of a drawing. Using both will give your drawings character.

The term value is sometimes used interchangeably with the terms "shade", "tint" and "tone." These terms are most useful when working with colored pencils.

Shade refers to the color achieved when black is combined with a pure color. You can do this to darken colors. For example, ultramarine, navy blue and midnight blue are shades of blue.

Tint refers to the color achieved when white is combined with a pure color. You can do this to lighten colors. For example, pink, rose and coral are tints of red.

Tone refers to the color achieved when grey is combined with a pure color. For example, khaki, brown and gold are tones of yellow.

However, when drawing with grey graphite pencils, these will all just fall under "value." Knowing if a color is a shade, tint or tone will allow you to adjust the values in your drawings to depict the color of your subject even in a black and white drawing. You simply need to look at the darkness or lightness of the greys you are using. A pink-colored blouse will look like a light grey while dark blue denim jeans will look almost black.

Furthermore, take note that value is different from the concept of shading, which will be discussed in Chapter 4. So for this chapter, only look at the "color" of the lines you are making

Value Scale

A value scale is extremely helpful to beginner artists. This will serve as a guide so you can tell what value you can use for different parts of your drawing. Most find a ten-point value scale to be adequate. You can make one on a piece of paper by drawing ten circles or squares. Fill the first one with the lightest stroke you can create with your pencil or with your lightest pencil. Next, fill the last one with the darkest stroke you can create with your pencil or with your darkest pencil.

Fill the rest with the remaining values in between going from the lightest to the darkest value. Use this scale as a guide that you can compare parts of your drawing to, so the heaviest outline should match the last value while faint edges should match the first value. Medium colors should match the two middle values.

By using values, you can also adjust the contrast of your drawing. A high contrast drawing will make more use of values at each end of the spectrum - almost black to almost white. Low contrast drawings will use a good mix of the whole spectrum. Whichever variation in value that you choose is completely up to you and will depend on the effect that you want to achieve. Your drawing can be harsh, bold and solid or soft, faint and hazy.

Thick and Thin Lines

The quickest way to achieve various values in your drawing is to vary the thickness of your lines. Thin lines represent the light values while thick lines represent the dark values. You can get different thicknesses by simply varying your pressure, using pencil points with different dullness, or using different pencils.

Scribbling

Scribbling is a good way to fill a space with a lot of values in a short period of time. It is quick and you can create hundreds of strokes in a minute. More advanced artists can create drawings made up of just scribbles and the subject will still remain clear to the viewer. Beginner artists may try this technique and just end up with a bunch of scribbles that do not look like anything. Again, focusing on the shape of the subject will give you a general guideline for where to lay down the scribbles on your paper.

You do scribbling by drawing a continuous series of lines that go in different directions. The sensation you should feel when scribbling is comparable to writing in longhand or cursive. Control the value by varying speed, pressure and distance between the scribbles. For example, when doing a portrait using the scribbling technique, the dark and closely overlapping scribbles will be concentrated on the subject's features like his hair, eyebrows, eyes, nose, mouth and general outline of the face.

Some scribbles may be used to define cheekbones, the sides of the nose and around the mouth where shadows fall on the face. Lastly, very faint scribbles can depict highlights on the face like the apples of the cheeks, the pupil and whites of the eyes, and shine of the lips and hair.

Side Strokes

Side strokes is a favorite among sketchers who do fast and loose drawings. They are especially good for achieving different values than for plain contour drawings. Short, sideways strokes will create different values of greys depending on the pressure, closeness of the lines and overlapping.

Wide Strokes

Wide strokes are good if you want to try getting a general impression of a subject. You use big, long (not necessarily dark) lines. Whereas side strokes are short lines, wide strokes take up more space in a short period of time. So, they are often used for large subjects like the full figure of a person or a wide landscape. You can also use them when getting the general movement or shape of a large portion of the drawing such as the drape of a fabric or hair flowing in the wind. It takes a lot of confidence to achieve wide strokes because it can sometimes make or break the foundation of your entire drawing.

Charcoal pencils or pastels are great to use when trying to achieve wide strokes, because these take less effort to get broad lines. They also go on paper smoothly and don't catch on the "teeth" of the paper, which sometimes happens when drawing wide strokes with graphite pencils.

Single Strokes

Single strokes are simply straight lines drawn in a row. This is best done with a sharp pencil and each area is filled with parallel lines. Values are achieved by varying the density of the lines or how close the group of lines are to each other. The farther away the lines are, the lighter the value. It is a refined technique and is not as loose as the previous types of line drawings. It does create a similar effect with scribbling, except more polished.

However, it takes precision because one line that is not in its right place or a bit more crooked than the other will easily stand out and catch the attention of the viewer. Beginner artists should practice using this technique just to learn patience and meticulousness in drawing. It is good to use as a counter-balance to other stroke techniques. It is also best used for drawings that require precision like architecture.

Smudging and Erasing

After scribbling or doing side strokes, you can smudge the lines with your finger or other blender tools mentioned in Chapter 1. This will soften or smoothen the harsh lines. It is also a good technique to use when trying to achieve medium values. However, some artists avoid this technique because it does not teach how to achieve values properly using only lines. Also, smudging can get quite messy, which can ruin an already good drawing. It may be a form of cheating, but when done right or with some caution, you can enhance the drawing.

Another way to achieve lighter values is by erasing. This creates highlights or contrasting definition to some parts of a drawing. Sometimes, it is easier to just erase a portion filled with darker values than to avoid drawing on that spot or trying to achieve the lightest value you can.

Chapter 5 - Easy Technique 2 - Shading

Shading is another important technique in drawing. They give your sketches life and depth because they mimic the light and shadows found in the real world.

The progression of shading or values from light to dark or dark to light are called graduations. Graduated shading is important so that there is a good transition from one value to another. Beginner artists may jump from one value to another without proper graduation and this creates harsh, unrealistic shadows in their drawings. This is only acceptable when one is trying to create an obvious contrast between different portions of a drawing. For instance, the edge of an object should be distinguishable from its background; otherwise, the object will disappear.

Graduations can be done through a variation of strokes, pressure or pencil hardness. Continuously adjust the changes in values so that the transitions are not apparent. There should be no demarcations or borders that separate two or more values in a graduated shading. Adjust any areas that look irregular.

If you are just starting to experiment with graduation in drawing, you should being from the lightest shading to the darkest. It is much easier to build up on the color of a grey pencil than it is to remove an already dark color to make it lighter.

Light Source

Always identify where the light source of your subject is. When you do not consider where the light is coming from, your drawing will look two dimensional. For example, when drawing an outdoor scene, take note of where the sun is depending on the time of day. Noon time creates solid shadows that are short and go straight down from the objects. The lower the sun in the sky is (especially at the beginning and at the end of the day), the longer and fainter the shadows are. They will also slant at different directions. When it comes to drawing still life indoors, take notice of where the window is or where a light fixture is in a room - those are your possible sources of light.

Use the light as a guide where to draw shading, so a circle can transform in a sphere. Amateur artists will just place shadows and highlights where they think it looks good, so then, the drawing will turn out looking wrong. It is not as simple as coloring in a drawing, especially when only working with grey pencils.

A drawing can also have multiple sources of light. The closer or stronger the light source is, the darker the shadows and the lighter the highlights will be. That is another reason why artists should start with drawing objects from the real world. Understanding how light affects how an object looks is important in accurately capturing it on paper. Always pay close attention to the object you are drawing, including the different factors that surround it.

Highlighting

Highlights are parts of an object where bright areas form as a light hits it. The part, which is most directly hit by the light source will then be the brightest, thus, you need to shade them with light values. This should be the portion closest to the light. An apple directly under a light bulb will have a highlight on its top portion that graduates as you move down to the bottom of the apple where you will find the shadow. As such, highlights accentuate the form of an object because it can depict where an object bulges or where parts of it protrude.

In portrait drawings, the highlights are often found on the tip of the nose, the apples of the cheeks, the forehead, the chin and the Cupid's bow. The texture of an object will also affect how highlights look on it. For instance, shiny surfaces like glass, water or a person's eyes will catch light better than coarser surfaces like sand, carpeting or wood. Also, the color of an object affects how well it can reflect light back to the viewer.

Light-colored or white-colored objects generally reflect light better while dark-colored objects absorb light, so light green leaves on a tree will have lighter highlights than the dark wood of its trunk. However, the contrast between the highlight and the rest of the object can also be more apparent in dark-colored objects. For instance, highlight on brunette hair is more obvious than on blond hair.

The value of a highlight also varies depending on the type of highlight that an object receives. A highlight formed from the direct light of a source should be bright. However, highlights can also form from indirect reflections or bouncing of light around the object. For example, the shiny surface of an apple can bounce a tiny bit of light on objects surrounding it. Their highlights will be faint, but these should still be depicted to create more realistic representations of the objects.

Casting Shadows

Shadows are found in the parts of a drawing that receive the least amount of light. It can also be found when parts of an object block the light such as in creases and dips. Things surrounding that object can also block light or cast a shadow depending on the angle that the light is coming from. These are then shaded with the darker values, so the top of an apple right under a bright light will still have dark shading where you can find the stem. In portrait drawings, shadows can be found on the parts of the face obscured by hair, the inside of the mouth, the cheekbones, under the eyebrows and eyes, and the creases in the ears, around the eyes and mouth.

Just like in highlighting, the natural color and texture of an object will also affect the shadows that form on it. For example, a long-haired fur coat on a dog will create a lot of small shadows where the tiny hairs are located. The shadow on a black t-shirt will also have to be much darker than when drawing shadows on a white t-shirt where it more easily shows up.

A shadow should also be graduated and should not simply appear as black shading. The portions of a shadow farther away from where an object obstruct light should be lighter, so the long shadow of a tree will be darkest near the roots and fade to a lighter value as it moves away from the roots. This also suggests the placement of objects in your drawing and creates the illusion of depth and perspective.

Shadows also suggest the parts of objects that are touching or are close to one another. Instead of drawing sharp edges, an object's edges can be more realistically depicted through the use of shadows.

Reflected light also affects how shadows look. The form of an object can be further enhanced by looking at where light is reflected from other objects. This goes in tandem with highlighting. Once you understand how highlighting and shadowing works, you can create three dimensional realities in your drawings.

Hatching

Hatching is a set of straight or curved lines drawn in a series beside each other to achieve a particular value. This is a common shading technique and is the easiest to master. That is because you are only working with one set of hatches. The density of the hatches will create the effect that you want, so hatching sets close to one another will look darker while hatching sets that are far apart will look lighter. Very close hatching lines will create the illusion of a solid value or color.

The hatches can also be short or long depending on the area that the artist wants to cover. For example, a shadow cast by a pine tree will form a triangular shape. So, the hatches can be a series of short and long lines that form the rough shape of a triangle. Hatching is also commonly used to draw straight hair or fur.

You can achieve graduation by changing the thickness of the lines and the distances between them. The principle is similar to some stroke techniques discussed in the previous chapter.

Crosshatching

Crosshatching is a type of hatching where the hatching sets are laid on top of one another as if creating crosses. When you overlap two or more hatching sets, you can create darker values. However, crosshatched sets with hatching sets that are far apart will show up as lighter values. The form of crosshatched sets usually follows the shape of an object to depict creases and textures. It is often used to show shadows on an object and does not have to rely on an outline. The spaces in between the hatches can be apparent or they can look like a solid shade depending on the effect that the artist wants to achieve.

Scribbling

Scribbling can also be a shading technique, especially when used in overlapping sets to create different values. It is a versatile technique that you can use to create shading on textures like curly hair, grassy fields or fuzzy cloth. The texture of scribbles can be adjusted to depict the smoothness or roughness of a surface. Scribbles and be a series of squiggles, entwined circles or irregular continuous lines. When used properly by more advanced artists, scribbling can still look quite polished rather than look like a random, unfinished doodle.

Dots

Dots are technically small lines or points. You can use them for shading through a variation of density and pressure. In essence, a densely grouped set of heavily drawn dots will look darker than a group of light dots drawn far apart. It does take a longer time to shade using dots than with other shading techniques, but the payoff can well be worth it. The illusion can be interesting for the viewer especially for larger art pieces. The nearer the viewer is, the more he or she will be able to appreciate the effort that went into the drawing.

A type of drawing that uses dots exclusively is called pointillism. Every dot is laid dot one by one to create lines, forms and shapes.

You can also cheat with this technique by holding several pencils together to draw multiple dots at the same time. It may be less precise, but it does cover more area in a shorter period of time. This technique is sometimes called stippling.

Chapter 6 - Easy Technique 3 - Proportion

Proportion is another important element of any good drawing. Many drawings with good lines and shading still look odd because they do not follow the right proportions. Think of a room filled with people. You may think that all the people in that room are the same size, so you will draw them that way. However, a room is not a flat like a piece of paper. People will stand in different places with some closer to the viewer than others, so those who are closest to you should look bigger than those standing in farther parts of the room.

Also, their sizes and shapes will depend on which direction of the room you are looking towards. If you are looking slightly upwards to the ceiling while sitting down on the floor, then the people's legs will look bigger than their heads, even though common sense dictates that legs should be smaller than heads. This distortion is due to different factors that affect proportion.

Depth of field

Any three dimensional drawing will have different depths of field. There should at least be a foreground, middle ground and background and objects should be found on these different levels. This tricks the viewer's eye into thinking that he or she is not looking at a flat piece of paper but rather, a 3-dimensional picture.

As such, the placement of objects on these different levels of depth of field will affect their size and shape. The objects closest to the viewer should appear biggest while the objects farthest from the viewer should appear smallest. Their sizes relative to one another in the drawing will also be affected by the distances between these levels and the actual sizes of the objects. For instance, a large mountain can still appear quite large even when it is in the background of a drawing, granted that the distance of the mountain is not that far from the viewer. A bird in the foreground will still look quite small compared to other objects in a landscape drawing because birds really are small in real life.

Foreshortening

Foreshortening refers to the shortening of an object as it moves towards the viewer. For instance, imagine a person with one arm by his side and another arm reaching out towards you. The arms on an average person should be the same length, but when drawing arms at different distances from the viewer, the arm closer to you should look shorter but bigger. This suggests that the arm is in the foreground while the other arm is located farther in the drawing.

The same principle applies when drawing any object that occupies different depths of field. For instance, you may be drawing a picture of a car from its front. The front of the car including its hood, front window and headlights should look big but short while its rear end should taper longer and look smaller.

By using foreshortening, you can also create the illusion of using different "lenses" in your drawing much like in photography. For example, a fish eye lens distorts an image in such a way that the center is larger and shorter than the rounded edges. You can use this when drawing reflections on concave surfaces like balls or windows or when depicting objects inside glasses like fishbowls and eyeglasses.

Similarly, wide-angle lenses also distort an image so that the central objects look large and shortened compared to the sides. You can use this technique when trying to depict objects that should look extremely close to the viewer like a very close-up shot of a person's face or a focal building surrounded by other minor buildings in an urban landscape.

Focal Point

The focal point is also important to consider when trying to get the perspective of a drawing correctly. This is the point where the viewer's eye is focused. Understand that your eyes can only point in one direction and on only one spot in a scene. That is why there are points in a scene that we call blind spots - spots that your eyes cannot see. To create realistic drawings, you can also mimic the illusion of peripheral vision.

To find the focal point of a drawing, just choose one spot to focus on in a scene. This can be found on any level of depth of field. However, beginner artists may want to start with a focal point somewhere in the middle ground or foreground and somewhere to one side of the scene. In a room, this can be the corner of one of the far walls. In a landscape, this can be the tip of a mountain. Also, take note that your focal point will be the focus of your drawing. It is one part where the eyes of the viewer will be drawn to, so choose a significant portion of the scene, usually one where the main subject is located.

Next, imagine lines radiating from that focal point. You can also draw these lines as your first layer of outlines as explained in Chapter 4. These lines will serve as guidelines for foreshortening your objects. Lines that radiate farther apart from one another should have shorter and bigger objects while lines that radiate closer to each other should contain longer and smaller objects.

Finding the focal point is much easier when drawing large scenes that contain different objects. It is a lot harder when drawing single subject accompanied by not a lot of objects. Sometimes, the focal point is already that one subject. This usually happens in portrait drawings, so just focus on one striking detail on the person's face like the lips or eyes then use shading and highlighting to emphasize that feature. It is always better to draw the viewer's gaze to one point in the drawing than to have a lot of things going on in a picture.

Grid Method

Drawing: 1-2-3 Easy Techniques to Mastering Drawing

For more accurate perspectives and scale, you can try the grid method when drawing. The grid method involves drawing as grid or a series of squares that will serve as guide when you are drawing a subject. These squares are of equal ratio and can be part of your first layer of outlines. They are usually erased before the drawing is finalized.

You can draw a rough grid on your paper by first finding the middle. Draw a vertical line and a horizontal line that meets in the middle of the paper, then divide the rest of the paper into equal parts. You can also use a ruler or straight edge to create a more precise guide. Some people may prefer to fold their paper in equal parts to create a sort of invisible grid without drawing any lines on the paper. However, you may find that the folds on the paper can still be distracting and may make it difficult to draw lines and shading more smoothly. This trick is best done on thin paper where folds can be smoothed out.

Then, imagine these lines over the subject you are drawing. They will allow you to find the correct placement of objects as well as their proper proportions relative to one another. It is best to start in the middle of the scene and work your way around the rest of the image. You are essentially filling out each box with a part of the image much like a jigsaw puzzle being put together. Be aware of the whole image that you are producing because if you focus on individual portions of the drawing without considering the bigger picture, the parts may end up looking disjointed.

This technique is especially useful in portrait drawings because the average human face has perfect proportions. The middle of the grid will be the nose and the eyes and mouth are located on equal distances from the nose.

Your grid does not necessarily have to be flat. It can also form the shape of a sphere as when drawing a round human head or a globe. Images that form cylinders or other curved objects will also benefit from a more spherical grid. The middle of spherical grids can be a straight line if the viewer is looking the image straight on or a curved line if the viewer is looking at an angle.

The grid technique is also used in image transfers. This is another exercise that beginner artists can try. You can do this by taking a printed photo and drawing a grid over the image, then try copying the image by drawing a similar grid on your paper and simply sketching the image as an exact replica of the photograph. This may not teach you how to draw realistically because you are drawing from another flat image, but it will teach you how to make use of the grid technique. It is also great when you want to simply copy other two-dimensional images like cartoons or letterings.

Over time and after a lot of practice, you can simply imagine the grid on your paper without having to draw it as an outline.

Conclusion

Thank you again for downloading this book!

I hope this book was able to help you to master basic techniques in drawing and help you on your way to becoming an advanced artist who experiments with different media and art genres.

The next step is to practice, practice and practice! That is the only way you can be a better artist. Try out every single tip you encountered in this book and draw wherever you can - at home, in a café, or out on the street. In no time, you will find that you rarely even think of these "rules" anymore and the lines, shading and proportion comes naturally to you as an artist.

Finally, if you enjoyed this book, please take the time to share your thoughts and post a review on Amazon. It'd be greatly appreciated!

Thank you and good luck!

Book 2
Oil Painting

By Scott Landowski

1-2-3 Easy Techniques to Mastering Oil Painting!

Oil Painting: 1-2-3 Easy Techniques to Mastering Oil Painting!

Table of Contents

Introduction

I want to thank you and congratulate you for downloading the book, Oil Painting: 1-2-3 Easy Techniques to Mastering Oil Painting!

This book contains proven steps and strategies on how to overcome different challenges in oil painting. The step-by-step approach of this book will guide you in achieving a successful start in your oil painting practice.

This book covers the fundamentals of oil painting, the principles of mixing oil paint colors and developing an image. The simplified steps are a guarantee that even beginners will be able to relate with the process.

Thank you and we hope you enjoy this book.

Chapter 1. Oil Painting Overview

Oil painting has been around for centuries. It makes use of a kind of paint that has creamy and smooth consistency, and can produce vivid colors. When one speaks of oil painting, the image of great artists and their masterpieces also come to mind. This is a very old painting practice and though there have been a lot of changes in the materials being used, the techniques have not changed that much.

An oil paint consists of dry colored powder mixed with a drying oil as the binder; hence, the name. Some people create their own oil paints but you can buy ready to use oil paints from stores. Ready to use oil paints normally come in tubes. The oil paints are combined to make various colors.

Oil paints take time to dry. This attribute has its benefits and drawbacks. One of the benefits of using a slow drying paint is that you can refine and adjust the image that you are painting before it dries. Oil paints also make it possible for you to correct some parts of your painting that you want to remove. You can remove an image by using a wet rag, a palette knife or a rubber squeegee.

The disadvantage of using oil paints is that it can be difficult to apply different colors next to each because they can mix if you are not careful in applying them. Once a painting is finished and is completely dry a varnish is applied to protect the painting.

Mastering the art of chemistry is essential to achieving the proper effects for your work. This complexity of oil painting makes it fun and challenging to work with.

Basic Information About Painting Using Oil Paints

Most of the commercial tube paints are ready to use. In some instances, you may use a solvent or a medium to modify the paint. The solvent dilutes the paint and the medium adds oil back to the paint to make it creamy. As you spend more time working with oil paints, you will notice that some colors take more time to dry than the other colors.

After an oil paint, has been applied, it develops a skin of dry surface through the chemical process called curing. This process protects the surface of the painting. Take note though, that the surface might be dry but the entire painting itself will takes months before it becomes thoroughly dry.

You will also discover that two colors mixed together will not look the same if they are applied in two separate overlapping layers. This is the reason that at times, you will need to wait for the first layer to dry a bit before you apply the next layer to achieve a certain color or texture. It is important for a beginner to know these qualities of oil paints for a successful painting project.

Materials Used in Oil Painting

- **Oil Paints**
  Oil paint is a type of paint that consists of a colored powder mixed with a drying oil. The most popular drying oil is linseed oil. The drying oil makes the paint dry slowly. You can buy ready to use oil paints in various colors.
- **Viewfinder**
  A viewfinder is a sighting tool that helps you create a frame for your object, just like a viewfinder on a camera. You can make one by cutting a window out an index card. The outer layer will serve as your frame. The items you see inside its window will be the same item you will paint in your canvas.
- **Canvas**
  A canvas is commonly used fabric used for painting. The fabric is usually placed in a wooden frame.
- **Easel**
  It is a self-supporting wooden frame used to hold the canvas while it is being painted or drawn.
- **Palette**
  A palette is a thin board where oil paints are mixed. It can be made of wood, plastic, ceramic or other materials. It also comes in different sizes and shapes
- **Different sizes of paintbrush**
  A paintbrush has bristles, a handle, and a ferrule. Brushes come in different sizes, shapes and have different types of bristles.
- **Palette knife**
  The palette knife is a thin steel blade with a handle and is used for mixing colors and applying or removing paint.
- **Paint thinner, turpentine, solvent or linseed oil**
  These liquid materials are used to adjust the consistency of the oil paint.

Chapter 2. Fundamentals of Oil Painting

Before you start painting, familiarize yourself first with the basics of the painting process. This means that you should study the basic shapes and colors of an image before getting into the details.

Basic Painting Process

One of the main qualities of oil painting is applying paint in layers. The first step in oil painting is to sketch in the different parts of the painting using a wash. A wash is a pale color that is made by mixing an oil paint with a solvent.

After making the sketch, apply paint in the major light and dark areas. Adjust the colors and shapes by starting with a thin layer of paint. Gradually apply thicker layers of paint to let the colors in the lower layer's peek through.

Below is a more detailed instruction of the steps:

1. Create a sketch.
   The initial marks on a canvas make up the drawing using a wash. A wash is a thin mixture of paint and solvent that is fast drying and easy to modify. You can easily make changes to your drawing at this stage. Do not use a solvent to erase or clean marks because it will just create a mess. The best way to correct part of the sketch is to wait until it slightly dries and paint over it.

2. Choose your plot.
   After you outlined the image on the canvas, you will be able to foresee the outcome of your painting. At this stage, you should still be able to make changes and improve the overall design of your painting.

3. Apply the major colors.
   Once you have finalized your design, you can block in the major colors. You can adjust on the object of your painting as you apply the major colors. Your painting takes on a more substantial appearance as you apply more colors.

4. Paint in layers.

With the basic colors in place, you can start applying heavier paint to your objects. The succeeding layers can be of the same shade of color or you may adjust it to depending on the effect that you would like to bring out in the painting.

Brushes and Brushstrokes

Brushes come in different sizes and shapes. They are usually long enough to allow you to vary the brushstrokes just by changing the way you hold the brush. For instance, if you hold the brush down by the ferrule, you use the small muscles of your hand and fingers and have fine control over the strokes. On the contrary, if you hold the brush farther away from the ferrule, you have a looser hold on the brush for loose, expressive strokes. The ferule is the metal part of the paintbrush that olds the bristles and the handle together.

Different Brush Sizes and Bristles

- Short and square-ended paintbrush makes square corners and tight edges. This brush is great for geometric shapes or manmade objects.
- Long and floppy filberts make elegant, organic, lozenge-shaped marks. This brush is perfect for organic and natural objects.
- Sable or synthetic fibers are more delicate than the bristle brushes and leave less of a mark.

Different types of Paintbrush

1. **Filbert**
   Filberts are used this to paint leaves, clouds and other living things and natural organic forms.
2. **Flat**
   This paints large areas of color. This type of paintbrush is also best for painting geometric forms and filling out square corners because it gives a clean crisp edge.
3. **Bright**
   This brush is like flat the only difference is that it is shorter, broader and holds less paint.
4. **Round**

This is great for drawing lines.

5. **Fan brushes**

   The fan brushes are used for fine blending.

6. **Extra-long filberts**

   You can use these to make very loose and expressive marks.

7. **Stencil brushes**

   You can use a stencil brush for dry brush. They are chubby and round.

8. **House painting brushes**

   Use them for big projects and for dry brushing.

9. **Foam brushes**

   You can use them pick up excess paint.

10. **Painting knife**

    This like a palette knife but it is more rigid. You can use it as a trowel to pick up paint and apply it to the canvas.

Different Glazing Techniques

A glaze is a transparent coat applied to create an illusion of a third color. It is a thin layer applied over another color. Glazing refers to any type of painting that allows you to see two different colors at the same time. You can see this definition in layers of color thinned with medium. You can also see it when paint is marked in small spots of color.

- **Imprimatura**

  This Italian term means that you start with a colored background. The typical background of a painting is white. However, there are instances wherein you will start your painting with a colored canvas. If you have a colored canvas, paint it with a fast-drying coat to bring out the undertones. Allow the area to dry a bit before you wipe away some of the paint. Create the light areas of your image by wiping them with a rag or a dry paintbrush. Let it dry thoroughly before you proceed with your painting. This technique is like using an eraser to pull out the light areas of the drawing rather than laying in dark areas.

- **Scumbling**

  It refers to removing a thin layer of a paint by applying an oil paint on it. You scrape off the excess paint until just a tiny part of it is left. This technique works well with dense colors especially if a light color is applied over a dark color.

- **Sgraffito**

  This is like scumbling; the only difference is that with sgraffito distinct marks are left. You can use this technique if you want to show defined textures or ragged edges.

- **Dry Brush**

  This technique is done on a dry part of your painting. Lightly brush over the painting using a stiff, dried paint on a dry brush. This works best and produces more specks on a rough and textured surface rather than on a smooth surface.

- **Impasto**

  This is the process of painting using a thick paint. This helps to add texture to the painting. You can use a regular oil paint or a ready to use impasto medium.

Chapter 3. Master the Art of Mixing Colors

Mixing and matching colors can be overwhelming. Mixing colors is an essential technique that every beginner must learn. Most beginners think that the best way to make something look darker is to mix it with black and to make something lighter you mix it with white. These color combinations though will not help you achieve your desired color.

The best way to learn about colors is by creating a color chart and knowing the color wheel. That way, you will discover how to make light and darks using other colors instead of just using black and white. This technique will keep you from making the mistake that most beginners commit which is creating cloudy colors. By making a color chart or wheel, you will learn how to mix the colors and begin to get a feel for applying paint to the canvas in a uniform manner.

Color Terminologies

It is important that before you make a color wheel or chart, you are familiar with the color terminologies to avoid confusions.

- **Primary Colors**
  These are red, blue and yellow.
- **Hue**
  Hue is the name of the color, such as red, green, blue, or another color. A pure hue is the brightest version of a color.
- **Tint**
  A tint is a lighter version of a hue. You make a tint by adding white to a pure hue.
- **Shade**
  A shade is a mixture of the pure hue plus black. Another way to make a shade is to use the hue's complement rather than black in these mixtures.
- **Complement**
  It is the hue directly across the color wheel from the hue that you are working with.
- **Tone**

35

It is a mixture of a shade plus white, or you can think of it as the pure hue plus black and white. You can also use the complement rather than black in the mixture.

Color Illusions

Once you have mastered the color wheel and the art of mixing colors, you must also familiarize about the effects of colors with each other.

- **Value and Size**
  A color in a smaller area will seem darker and brighter. An example would be the color on the cover of a paint can, if you paint an entire room with it, you will notice that the color appears lighter compared to how it appears on the cover of the can. The smaller the area that a color covers, the darker it appears.

- **Value**
  A color surrounded by a lighter color appears to be darker, but if it is surrounded by a darker color, it appears to be lighter.

- **Hue Effect**
  A color surrounded by one of its primary hues appears to be more like its other primary pure hue.

  For instance, you want to use violet in a paint. Violet is made of the primary colors red and blue. If red surrounds a violet paint, the violet paint would look like it has more blue in it. On the contrary, if blue surrounds violet, the violet paint would appear as if it has more red in it. Though, the two violets are of the same concentration.

- **Intensity**
  Complementary colors placed next to each other make each other look brighter, but similar hues make each other look duller. On the other hand, any brighter color makes another color look darker, and any dark color makes another color look brighter.

Chapter 4. Monochromatic Painting

Start with Black and White Paint

Black and white painting is a type of monochromatic painting or also known as under-painting. Monochromatic painting just uses one color or hue but in ranging values, from light, medium to dark. In black and white painting, you use different values of gray (a combination of black and white) to create your painting.

Starting your oil painting adventure in black and white makes it less overwhelming. However, it's a good way to practice as it gives you the chance to use oil paints and see how they work. This exercise is like creating a sketch.

- **Find a Still Subject**
  Look for things that are plain and simple. Choose two to three items and group them together but do not place them tightly close to each other. Place your objects in an area that will let them cast shadows.
  Arrange your objects so that the areas around them make remarkable shapes as well.

- **Draw the Initial Sketch**
  Do not use a pencil to draw the sketch on your canvas. Use a wash or a pale paint to draw your sketch. A wash is a pale color of your paint. You can create a wash by directly mixing a pool of gray oil paint in a jar of a solvent.

  Another way is you squeeze out a pool of white and black paint on your palette. Then take a small part of your white and black paint using a palette knife to create a gray mixture. Dampen a round brush with a solvent and knock off the excess solvent. Take a small amount of the gray paint. You will still end up with a wash of gray because of the solvent on the brush.

Sketch your outline using the gray wash. If you need to make corrections, use a darker shade of gray.

- **Sighting and Measuring**
  Sighting is a way of checking to see whether your objects are drawn properly. You can use your paintbrush handle to compare the actual object to the painted object. You can do this by closing one eye and holding out your paintbrush handle at arm's length and visually lay it along the edge of the item to get the angle that you are trying to draw.

- **Block Major Shadows**
  Locate the shadows of your object. Dip a brush in solvent and take some of the gray wash used for the initial sketch. Apply paint on the dark side of the objects.

- **Develop the Image**
  The basic rule of painting is that you start with the main objects first and secondary areas like the shadow and then the background. When you develop the image, you need to mix three shades of gray and use a different paintbrush for it. Using a palette knife, create a light gray, medium gray, and dark gray. Apply the medium gray first on the middle areas. Use the light grey in areas that are closer to the light and the dark gray to the shadows. As you paint the entire canvass, you can make adjustments on your objects to achieve a more polished image. It is important not to leave any part of the canvass unpainted because it will eventually turn to yellow that would ruin the effect of your painting.

Chapter 5. Paint Local Colors Using Analogous Colors

Analogous means identical or similar. You can practice painting objects by finding its analogous color in the color wheel. It can be difficult to paint objects in colors particularly for beginners. For this painting, do not use black and white colors. You use complementary colors to make something appear darker.

To practice your painting skill, start with painting a green apple, an orange and a lemon. Objects that are medium or light in color are best for this exercise. For the background, use a blue cloth.

Frame and sketch

Use a viewfinder to frame your scene and sketch the objects using a wash. Make a wash of the color with your solvent, and use the wash to draw out the objects. Make the objects nice and big or at least life-size.

You can adjust your drawing by choosing a color slightly darker that the first. Using a different color helps you keep track of which line to use when you begin to develop the painting.

Find the local color

The local color is the natural color of an object as it appears in normal light. Look at the objects you have and ask yourself what colors they are. The green apple is more yellow-green than green; the orange is orange; and the lemon is yellow.

Paint the Orange

Now mix a small pool of color to match the local color of one of your orange. You may have to adjust the actual color by using more yellow or red to get the right color.

To match color perfectly, put some of your paint on your palette knife and place it next to the object. Make sure that you hold it up to the side of the orange that is closer to the light. If you see a color in the object that is missing on the knife, add that color. For example, if your orange fruit looks more yellow than the paint on the knife, add yellow; if it looks more reddish, add red. Experiment with the colors to get the right one. It takes practice to master color combination. Just try and try and add just a little bit at a time until you get it right.

1. **Choose analogous colors.**

Find the color that comes the closest to the color of the orange in your still life. In this case, it will be orange. Look also for tubes of oil paints that match the color of the other parts of your orange and put them on your palette as well. You do not have to mix anything at this point. Just place the oil paints next to each other in your palette. Squeeze out small amount of yellow, red, yellowish-brown, and crimson.

2. **Begin applying the color.**

Take the orange paint that you made and apply a thin wash to the orange on your canvas. Cover the middle and shaded side of the orange with this color. As you get to the part of the orange that is lighter, pick up some yellow with the same brush and add it right to the canvas. It will look yellow-orange. You can also add pure yellow to the exact point where the light hits the orange.

For the shaded side, make a color that is more red-orange. Use a fresh, clean brush to apply it to the underside of the orange on your canvas. Now your orange fruit is orange with yellow highlights and a red-orange shaded side. You can use a red that has a bit of crimson for the very bottom of the orange.

3. **Do not blend the colors in applying the paint instead apply them in a block.**

Paint the Lemon

The lemon is a little tricky because its local color is bright yellow. It is the lightest color on the color wheel, so it functions as the highlight. With yellow objects, you should figure out which direction to move on the color chart to find the analogous color to create a shadow of yellow that looks like it belongs on a lemon. Paint the entire lemon with yellow and then move on to the shaded side.

Your analogous color options are green and orange. When you look closely at the lemon on the shaded side, you notice that it looks greenish on the darker side. So, use yellow for the highlight and yellow-green for the shaded side. Experiment with different greens for your lemon.

Paint the Green Apple

The apple on your sketch will be round, but you know that the shape of an apple is significantly different from an orange. The stem comes out on the top through a hollow part.

Using a yellow wash for your drawing, adjust the shape of the apple. Find the little indention at the top of the apple, and use your yellow to make a mark. Change it with the next analogous color, like yellow-green. Use yellow to establish the structure of the apple by making a line right through the middle of the apple as if you are stabbing it. Draw an ellipse on the top of the apple and then make a second ellipse to mark the shoulders of the apple.

The local color of the green apple is yellow-green. The apple also has yellow highlights and a green-shaded side. Use yellow, and a tiny bit of both ultramarine blue and cerulean blue.

Find the shaded side and paint it in with a thin wash of yellow-green. Continue to fill in the lights with yellow and the shaded side with green. The green is in the top indention and off to one side of the indention. Use yellow or a lighter version of yellow-green to fill in the lightest part of the green apple.

The Background

Identify the local color of your cloth first and find its analogous color. Find all the blues, blue-greens, and blue-violets that may work for your cloth. The shadows cast by the objects onto the cloth are a darker version of the color of the cloth; they have nothing to do with the color of the object casting the shadow. Take the color of the cloth and the color for the cast shadows and apply them to the painting in a thin wash.

Paint Shiny Objects

You have learned previous how to apply colors. You already know how to use colors to create a three-dimensional form. However, you have yet to learn how to paint objects that are more complicated. These are the shiny objects like a metal and a glass. In painting a shiny object, you must learn how to capture its glimmer and glow.

Paint Metal

Start with a simple metal subject like a tin can. You can find it anywhere and it is very easy to draw in terms of shape. You can paint an image of the can by itself, or make a small still life with the can. Place the can on a surface with some color and experiment with the lighting and placement of other items around the can. The other object near the tin can will show their reflection on it. Place a brightly colored object nearby like a box, and play with the reflections.

Your still life set up should be about 2 to 4 feet away from you. You should have good lighting for the objects that you are painting. This painting takes more than just one session. Make sure that you can leave your setup in one place without having to move the items.

Steps to Draw the Tin Can

Start by drawing the tin can and any other objects in your setup on the canvas. Sketch the can, its cast shadow, and the box with light sketchy lines so that you could easily correct them.

Draw the tin can by making ellipses for the top and bottom and then connect them for the sides. This step uses the transparent construction method. The tin can be just a cylinder with ribs. You can make the ellipses by keeping your hand steady as you make a circular motion using your upper arm. Make several ellipses at the top and bottom part of the can.

Then draw the ones in between. Make sure to create an even space for the ribs. Keep your hand steady and try to mimic the ellipses that you drew for the top and bottom of the can. Draw the entire ellipse even though you see only the forward edge in the finished painting. When you fill in the other ellipses, they will look stacked. This creates the ribs of the can.

First Session

1. Find the patches of color.

   When you look at the can, you see gray, but you also see the reflection of other colors. Look at the shapes and patterns of the different values and colors in the can. Try to see it as a paint-by-number painting where you have larger shapes of color that break down into smaller shapes. In the tin, can, you also see bands of colors that move around its contour.

2. Apply the local colors that you see in a thin wash.

   The pattern of the ribs of the can should have light and dark colors which creates a series of dashes. Across the ribs of the can, they stack up like bricks. Do not blend colors, just paint by block using the patterns that you see on the can. Painting metal is about painting patterns. Painting without blending is what makes metal look like a metal.

3. As you paint, look at the can and examine the reflections that you see on its surface.

   Identify the items on the reflection to help you to help you identify the colors that you see on the can. Add the reflection in the dashes along the ribs and be sure to match the color to its nearby source.

4. Make alterations and continue to develop the patterns by using the colors that you see and add them in spots and patches. After you have all the colors blocked in, you can set the canvas aside to dry a little before you continue.

Second Session

After a day or two, you can continue with the next session. Some parts of the painting may feel completely dry while others may have started to develop a sticky surface. They will be wet again as soon as you add more paint. This allows you to blend and mix your colors right on the canvas.

Whenever you spend more than one session on a painting, you must use a drying oil medium rather than solvent. A painting medium allows the painting to dry properly. It adds back in a little of the linseed oil that the solvent dissolves out. It allows you to paint with smooth strokes and to blend and it slows the drying time of your painting. If an oil painting dries too quickly, it damages the layers of paint, causing the surface of the painting to crack.

You can make your own medium or you can use a commercially prepared painting medium. Use the painting medium to wet your brush as you work. The medium makes your paint fluid and creamy. It is very different from working with plain solvent, which can make your paint drippy and watery. The oil in the medium also helps to remoisten the previous layers, which allows the new layers to bond with the previous layers.

Continue to apply paint to the canvas, gradually building up the layers. Try to work with patches of color to develop, and refine patterns of value and colors as you work.

If you have an area that you should blend, experiment with blending in a finite area to get the hang of using the medium. Refrain from using blending if you can to help you maintain clear edges and convincing reflections.

Continue to apply a new layer of paint to all parts of the canvas, developing the image as you go.

Finish off the painting by adding the glints of light on the surface of the can. These glints are white and may stand up pinpoint-like from the metal. In creating these glints, just take up a little dab of something white – (even something slightly off-white would do) using a small dry, brush with no solvent on it at all. Just touch the brush to the point you need and leave it alone.

44

Paint Glass

A glass is a challenging object to paint for beginners because it is transparent yet it reflects image at the same time. It catches the light and reflects it back to you. It can also include dark spots. You can also pick up reflections on the surface of the glass from objects in the room.

To practice painting a glass, start with a simple object like a regular wine glass with no ornaments. Does the same thing as you would do before you start painting. Lay your object on a background and frame your still life using a viewfinder. Once you have framed your still life, sketch the bottle using a wash.

First Session

1. Find the three largest shapes in the glass, and draw them in.
   Sketch in only the largest shapes now. As you establish the major shapes in your glass, try to identify the sources of the reflections that you see. For instance, if you see the reflection of a box in your glass, notice how the glass distorts its shape.
   Try to maintain the same viewpoint to capture the shapes more easily. In painting glass objects, every time you move, the shapes of the reflections in your object change as well.

2. Mix washes for the color of the wine glass and the other parts of your setup area.
   Concentrate first on the largest shapes. Notice that some areas inside the wine glass are a mix of both the color of the wine glass and the color from behind it. Make up these colors and apply them as you see them.

3. After you block in the major shapes in the glass, find the medium shapes and then the smallest   shapes and block them in.

4. Continue to develop the other parts of the canvas so that you have a consistent surface over the whole painting.

Second Session

After a day or two, polish the application of color to the glass using a painting medium. You can apply a relatively thick application of paint to make your wine glass look more fluid and more glass-like. Find the highlights and apply them with tiny points of white paint. If a light reflection on the glass is relatively big, apply a big patch of white on it instead of tiny dots.

Chapter 6. Painting a Portrait

Painting a portrait is one of the most difficult things that you can do. You must be keen in observing the many details that a human face has. If you are unable to capture certain details of a human face, the result will not turn out like your subject.

Although painting portraits can be a bit frustrating in the beginning, with practice you can develop the skills necessary to create a true likeness.

Practice Sketching the Proportions of a Face

You might already be familiar on how you set the outline to check the proportion of a face. It starts with by drawing an oval shape. Then you divide it up for placement of the eyes, nose, mouth, and so on. If you have never tried making a portrait before, you can practice drawing the features of the face first. You can start by drawing the different features of the face. You can draw from photos or from your image in the mirror. Practice drawing eyes, noses, and mouths until you feel comfortable with them.

You can start practicing the proportions of the face by following the steps:

1. Get a real-life picture of a person. You can use your own picture if you want. Just make sure that picture is life size or big enough for you to see the details.

2. Draw an oval on the canvas and look at the picture.

3. To measure the head, take one of your long paintbrushes and put the handle right down the middle of the face, touching the nose. The top end of the brush must stop exactly at the point at the top of the head. Get the measurement from the top of the head until the bottom part of the chin. You can use a ruler, if you find it more comfortable.

4. To find the eye level, measure from top of the head to the middle place between the eyes. Mark your eye level on your oval.

5. Place the handle so that it measures from your eye level to the chin and find the point for the base of the nose; mark this point on the oval.

47

6. Do the same for the position of the mouth, using the opening of your mouth as the measuring point.

Find the best point of view for a portrait

Portraits come in different positions and different styles. You will see some portraits wherein the head of the person is slightly tilted to one side, and some with just the face; others include the full body, and the list goes on.

Here are three of the most commonly used types of portraits that you can choose from:

- **Profile Portrait**
  A profile is the easiest point of view to portray, because most of the resemblance depends in the contour of the face. Profile paintings are more like mug shots but profile portraits generally do not include the front face. The main concern of the profile is face of the person

- **Full-face Portrait**
  The face of the person portrayed is directly facing the viewer. This type of portrait is the most difficult because the nose is directly pointing at the viewer, which makes it very hard to capture.

- **Three-quarter View Portrait**
  Three-quarter view is falls between the profile and the full-face portrait. This makes the subject look more natural.

For a beginner, the best option among the three would be the three-quarter view. To practice in painting a portrait, it will be best to start drawing a portrait of yourself. All you need is a mirror and you can position yourself in any way you want.

So, to start this activity, place the brush before your nose and turn your head a quarter. For this exercise, turn to your left. Notice how the eye, nose, and mouth level are the same, but your centerline is off to one side. Your centerline is curve and it follows the contours of the face. This curving line starts in the middle of your forehead and ends in the middle of your chin. It gently bends to the left to follow the line of the nose. The right cheek is a wide surface, but the left cheek is reduced.

Find the relative position of your facial features using your paintbrush handle. Hold it horizontally or vertically and see what parts of your features line up with others.

A Self-Portrait in Black and White

It is a good start to learn and study portraits by drawing a self-portrait because you get to paint whenever you want and virtually wherever you are.

Now the reason that you should start with black and white self-portrait is to simplify things. Master first the art of drawing the different features of your face and then just worry about adding the right colors later.

Work through the following steps to get started:

1. Gather your supplies.
   You need a canvas that is big enough to paint life-size face, a mirror, black and white paint, different types of paintbrush, solvent in a couple of jars, a palette, and a palette knife.

2. Set up your mirror and materials.
   Make sure that you have a three-quarter view of yourself in the mirror. Position a clear light source directed at your face from the side. You need a light source to see the contours of your face. A lamp or a bright window works well.

3. Create your wash.
   Mix up some light gray paint to make a wash and draw an oval on your canvas. Draw the proportions of your face. Your oval must be of the same size as your face to make it easier for you to paint.
4. Make a light line for the level of the eyes, nose, and mouth, and draw the location of the hairline. Check your work and make any necessary corrections.

Draw the big contour of the face

After drawing in the proportions of your face, draw a line for the outline that you see on the far side of the face. This contour line is important for finding the placement of the facial features. Follow these steps to find the outline of your face:

1. Begin from the top of the forehead, and curve the line outward to the brow.

2. Dip the line in to follow the hollow of your eye socket.

3. Make a curve line out for the cheekbone and down along the line of the cheek then gently curve in to the chin.

4. Connect the line of the chin in to join the neck. Do not worry if the chin extends beyond the initial oval that you drew.

Fill in the back of the head

The next step is to add some volume to the back of the head.

1. Draw a circular shape from the top of the head near the hairline. Make sure that the line will connect the head with the bottom of the ear. Just make an approximate line of your hair hides this part of your head.
2. Line up this point to the level of the lip line to be more precise.
3. Draw in the outline of the neck under the chin and draw another line from the back of the head.

Work on the contour of the nose

Create the outline of your nose by making another line with your wash. You draw this from your left eyebrow to the base of your nose.

Follow the steps to draw the contour of your nose:

1. Start at the point that is close to the contour of the side of your face. This is the part where the eyebrow extends the farthest.

2. Follow the contour of your eyebrow to the bridge of your nose. Then continue down to the angle of the nose until you reach base of your nose.

3. Add your philtrum. The philtrum is the vertical indentation between the base of the nose and the border of the upper lip.

Add in the features

Now, you add and enhance the other features of the face like the eyes and the mouth. When you draw an eye, the shape resembles to an almond with a round dark shade in the middle and a black dot for the pupil. However, the shape of the eyes look different in a three-quarter portrait which means that you also need to have a different approach to capture them.

Below are the steps to draw an eye for a three-quarter view:

1. Locate the iris of the eye on the far side of your face and put it in using the contour of the nose to help you place it. Your iris should appear as if it is tucked into the bridge of your nose.

2. Then draw your eyelids exactly as how they appear.

3. Draw a line to help you locate the corner of the lips. The far side of your lips should be smaller and the nearside will appear to be a bit bigger.

4. Find the points for the corners of the mouth, and then locate the centreline. Connect the two corners of your mouth using a line. The centerline of your mouth is a continuation of the philtrum.

5. Use the near corner of your lips as a guide to line up the position of the near eye. The corner of the near eye is above the corner of the mouth.

6. To help you find the width of your near eye, measure the base of the nose and the width of the mouth.

7. Check the position of your own face and make necessary adjustments on your painting to refine your features.

Develop the lights and darks of your face

1. Mix three pools of gray paint in different values. You must have a mixture of light gray, medium gray and dark gray. Use a different brush for each mix to avoid color contamination.
2. Find the shaded or dark part of your face and paint the dark gray in those areas.
3. Find the lightest areas of your face gray and paint them with the light gray. Do not blend, just work up the face in patches of light and dark gray.
4. Fill in the middle tones using the medium gray.
5. Cover the rest of the face with the appropriate grays.

Colored Self-Portrait

There are different types of skin tone and every individual has a different skin tone.

Flesh Tones

The human skin has the colors of the primary colors. As you work with oil paints, you will find out that a natural brown is a product of blues, yellows, and reds mixed in the right proportions. You can come up with various skin colors by varying the ratio of the three primary colors, and adding white.

Below are the colors mainly used for flesh skin tones:

- **Yellow**
  Yellow is widely used painting portraits. If you want dark skin, you may use raw or burnt umber.
- **Red**
  Crimson works best for a dark skin tone while red is best for a florid complexion.
- **Blue**
  Deep blue dulls the brilliance of the orange and when you mix the blue and orange, the hue would look for natural.
- **Titanium white**
  When it comes to skin tones titanium white is the best white to use.

Skin Formula

The skin has two basic tones: the light tone and the dark tone. Once you know the basic color combinations that make up these tones, it will be easy for you to come up with a more natural-looking skin.

- **Lighter Skin Tone Formula**

  Start by creating bright orange or you use a ready to use orange oil paint. To create a bright orange, mix yellow and red. Compare the shade of orange with the skin tone you are painting to see if you need to add more yellow or more red. You can adjust the hue by adding white to achieve a tone similar you what you see on a real person, with the lower portion of the check or and the inside of the arm lighter. You will notice that the mixture will be very light and odd to be a skin color. Now to make it look more like a natural skin color, you can add blue.

- **Darker Skin Tone Formula**

  Start with an orange oil paint. You can use an oil paint straight from a tube but the thing about it is, you will still be needing to make adjustments to it anyway so might as well just mix your own orange color. Compare your orange to the skin tone that you are painting. Check if they both lean toward yellow or red.

  Add blue to darken a skin tone or tones you can also try raw and burnt umber. Again, for lighter more natural-looking color, you can add white.

You will notice the colors used for both light and dark tones are the same. The only difference between the two is the ratio of the colors used.

One of the common mistakes of beginners is that they rely too much on white to achieve a light skin tone. When one uses too much white it makes the skin tone too pale and looks unnatural. Adding orange to it makes it more natural looking.

Normally the color of the skin of a person changes when exposed to a bright light. The color of the skin is warmer when it is lighter and cooler when it is darker. Therefore, when you paint a portrait of a person, you might just be using one tone but it will have different values as well.

Since you have already practiced how to make a self-portrait in black and white and you already know the basic formula for skin tones, you can now start making a colored self-portrait. Incorporate everything that you have learned from blocking in the shaded part of the painting to mixing colors and making a self-portrait.

You should also be more confident now to try other objects for your next oil painting project. Incorporate everything that you have learned in this book. Apply the basic knowledge in blocking in the shaded part of an object, different glazing techniques to make corrections, and using complimentary colors to add more complexity to your painting.

Conclusion

Thank you again for downloading this book!

I hope this book could help you gain confidence in trying oil painting. With everything that this book has imparted you, oil painting should no longer scare or intimidate you.

The basic techniques, discussed in this book should help you resolve your reservations in oil painting. It might be a complicated process but with sufficient knowledge and continuous practice, becoming comfortable with it is not impossible.

The next step you need to do is to buy your supplies and start painting.

Finally, if you enjoyed this book, please take the time to share your thoughts and post a review on Amazon. It'd be greatly appreciated!

Thank you and good luck!